D1161065

Julian Assange

Founder of WikiLeaks

Kristin Thiel

Cavendish Square

New York

Published in 2019 by Cavendish Square Publishing, LLC
243 5th Avenue, Suite 136, New York, NY 10016

First Edition

Website: cavendishsq.com

This publication represents the opinions and views of the author based on his or her personal experience, knowledge, and research. The information in this book serves as a general guide only. The author and publisher have used their best efforts in preparing this book and disclaim liability rising directly or indirectly from the use and application of this book.

All websites were available and accurate when this book was sent to press.

Library of Congress Cataloging-in-Publication Data

Names: Thiel, Kristin, 1977- author.
Title: Julian Assange : founder of Wikileaks / Kristin Thiel.
Description: New York : Cavendish Square, 2019. | Series: Hero or villain? : claims and counterclaims | Includes bibliographical references and index. | Audience: Grade 7-12.
Identifiers: LCCN 2017049415 (print) | LCCN 2017051369 (ebook) | ISBN 9781502635174 (library bound) | ISBN 9781502635198 (pbk.) | ISBN 9781502635181 (ebook)
Subjects: LCSH: Assange, Julian,--Juvenile literature. | WikiLeaks (Organization)--Juvenile literature. | Leaks (Disclosure of information)--Political aspects--Juvenile literature. | Whistle blowing--Political aspects--Juvenile literature.
Classification: LCC JF1525.S4 (ebook) | LCC JF1525.S4 T54 2019 (print) | DDC 025.06/30092 [B] --dc23
LC record available at https://lccn.loc.gov/2017049415

Editorial Director: David McNamara
Editor: Michael Spitz
Copy Editor: Rebecca Rohan
Associate Art Director: Amy Greenan
Designer: Amy Greenan/Christina Shults
Production Coordinator: Karol Szymczuk
Photo Research: J8 Media

Printed in the United States of America

CON TENTS

Julian Assange holds a United Nations report saying he was being wrongly detained in England.

A Man and a Mission: Setting the Stage

Julian Assange was born in 1971 in Australia. Though he and his family moved a lot and he didn't attend a traditional school until he enrolled (for a brief time) in college, in many ways, he was a regular kid: he was interested in exploring and learning new things. That curiosity, as well as his intelligence, led him toward computer programming and coding during the dawn of the internet age in the late 1980s and early 1990s. He focused his work through the lens of his belief that corporate and government transparency is key to a healthy society—in other words, secret documents shouldn't be secret; the details of major decisions should be shared with the public. This led him to a very irregular adulthood, one of power and infamy. In 2006, Assange founded WikiLeaks, an organization that publishes previously classified information, as well as analysis of those documents, videos, and other materials. The information it releases affects lives and changes recorded history.

Since the organization's official launch in 2006, WikiLeaks has been bound up together with Assange's public perception. Assange's story is WikiLeaks' and vice versa. Even Assange's cat is not separate from WikiLeaks. Michi, Cat-stro, or Embassy Cat, the name his furry friend goes by on Twitter, tweets about being a #whiskerblower and participating in "counter-purrveillance" (puns on "whistle-blower" and "countersurveillance").

Early Life

Assange grew up primarily in rural, coastal Australia. He didn't attend school but was instead both homeschooled by his mother and self-taught. When he wasn't at the library, he was running along the beach, building rafts, and riding horses. Not content to explore at just one level, he also climbed down into abandoned tunnels and mines, inventing his own adventures underground as well as above.

The World of Hacking

As a young teenager, he discovered yet another seemingly infinite playground to navigate. He began hacking into computer systems and networks. This opened up a whole new world—one made not of books or dirt or branches, but of electronic data and other information.

Julian Assange's cat is a popular resident of the Ecuadorian embassy in London.

Assange's first online handle was Mendax. He was sixteen years old and teaching himself computer programming. He was a voracious learner in all subjects, and the writing of ancient Roman poet Horace came to mind when he sat down to give himself a nickname to use while communicating online. Horace had written of *splendide mendax*, which means "nobly false" and "untruthful for a good cause," and, interestingly, that stuck with Assange.

All of this—his unconventional childhood and his incredible acumen, or skill, with computer programming and hacking—led him to create an organization that seeks to tear down hierarchies, bureaucracies, and closed doors by sharing classified or private documents and images. WikiLeaks doesn't redact the documents it receives before it sends them on to media sources. To remove or hide any piece of information in a document, even a person's credit card number or home address, would be seen by Assange as harming the integrity of the document, as CNET explained in a breakdown of WikiLeaks in 2017. The organization has been lauded with awards and nominations for honors, but it's also been the recipient of sanctions and backlash. For years, the major credit card companies refused to process

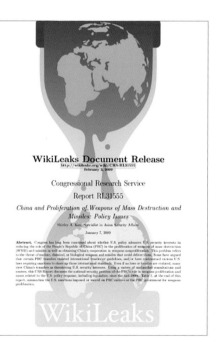

WikiLeaks Document Release
http://wikileaks.org/wiki/CRS-RL31555
February 2, 2009

Congressional Research Service

Report RL31555

China and Proliferation of Weapons of Mass Destruction and Missiles: Policy Issues
Shirley A. Kan, Specialist in Asian Security Affairs

January 7, 2009

Abstract. Congress has long been concerned about whether U.S. policy advances U.S. security interests in reducing the role of the People's Republic of China (PRC) in the proliferation of weapons of mass destruction (WMD) and missiles as well as obtaining China's cooperation in weapon nonproliferation. This problem refers to the threat of nuclear, chemical, or biological weapons and missiles that could deliver them. Some have argued that certain PRC transfers violated international treaties or guidelines, and/or have contravened various U.S. laws requiring sanctions to show up these international standards. Even if no laws or treaties are violated, many view China's transfers as threatening U.S. security interests. Using a variety of unclassified consultations and sources, this CRS Report discusses the national security problem of the PRC's role in weapon proliferation and issues related to the U.S. policy response, including legislation, since the mid-1990s. Table 1, at the end of this report, summarizes the U.S. sanctions imposed or waived on PRC entities or the PRC government for weapons proliferation.

WikiLeaks publishes a variety of previously secret documents.

donations to WikiLeaks, which uses such financial gifts to maintain its operations.

A lot has changed in the Australian's life in the thirty-some years since Assange used the handle Mendax, which mixed "good" and "bad" in its meaning. A lot of people still consider him as a blend of hero and villain.

Hero or Villain?

In 2012, Assange went into hiding, but in plain sight: as a political asylum seeker of the Ecuadorian embassy in London, England. Criminal charges in his personal and professional lives threatened his freedom, so he asked the Ecuadorian government to house him and protect him from authorities. He continues to be in the spotlight because he remains the leader of his headline-making organization— and also because he has such a big personality. A *New Yorker* journalist who has spent time with Assange over the years has called his character "complicated," explaining: "He is not merely the kind of person who will wear socks with holes; he is the kind of person who will wear socks with holes and rain fury upon anyone who mentions the holes in public." He holds the truth in the highest respect, but he "often appears to be unable to see past his own realities." He views humans as self-interested creatures, but WikiLeaks relies on individuals acting courageously and for some bigger purpose than themselves—regardless of whether a person "should" leak classified information to the public. To do so pits them against powerful governments, militaries, and corporations.

What Is WikiLeaks?

WikiLeaks is a multinational media organization and library whose employees analyze and publish restricted official materials, such as censored and confidential documents, involving war, spying, and corruption. As

WikiLeaks's logo shows the world dripping, or leaking.

of late 2017, it had released more than ten million documents and analyses. According to Assange, its founder, publisher, and spokesperson, in an interview with *Spiegel Online*, WikiLeaks is an "asylum" for "the world's most persecuted documents."

According to others, WikiLeaks is a journalistic organization, a group of whistle-blowers, or a collection of political actors—it's many things, depending on how each person is affected by the secrets it uncovers and shares. The organization has defined itself by its mission. When the organization was founded in 2006, its website said of its purpose, "The goal is justice. The method is transparency." In an interview with *Spiegel Online* nine years later, Assange amended that (or updated that a little): "To be honest, I don't like the word transparency; cold, dead glass is transparent. I prefer education or understanding, which are more human."

Collectively, WikiLeaks, its publisher, and its journalists have won many awards, including the *Economist* New Media Award (2008); *Time* Magazine Person of the Year, People's Choice (highest global vote) (2010); and the National Union of Journalists Journalist of the Year (Hrafnsson) (2011). They've been nominated for the UN Mandela Prize (2015) and the Nobel Peace Prize (2010–2015).

Foreign Minister Ricardo Patiño of Ecuador met with Julian Assange in London in 2013.

Assange continues to cultivate a curious response from people, and sometimes an angry one. The people closest to him, according to the 2017 *New Yorker* article, say that shouldn't be the media's focus. "Beyond the noise of his persona," they say, is a "technology that can be used for transformative good." Even if he were considered by everyone to be a mild-mannered hero, his work on its own would provoke some anger.

"The first casualty of war is truth"—that's a saying that Assange and WikiLeaks would agree with. When big, serious events happen, leaders may start bending and hiding the truth from the public. Assange and WikiLeaks believe they're here to push truth to center stage again. Any time someone stands up to those in power, that person will be both surrounded by cheerleaders and shouted down by critics. Assange's personal choices have also made people question whether he does more good than harm or more harm than good. The first thing to go in a complicated situation may be truth, but in the case of Assange and WikiLeaks, the truth itself is complex and unclear.

Daniel Ellsberg leaked what would become known as the Pentagon Papers.

Laws, Whistle-Blowers, and Technology: Before Assange and WikiLeaks

WikiLeaks has caused a splash in the news when it has published information, thanks in part to the world and times in which it operates. It is a twenty-first-century creation. The modern twenty-four-hour news cycle means that stories are covered around the clock. The internet and social media, available even in remote locations, allow people everywhere and anywhere to receive news as it's happening. Leaked information today affects a greater amount of people than ever before. Citizens, governments, and corporations of every country are tied together in the electronic age. When one group's action plans or even just gossip in the form of classified documents is leaked to the public, it matters to many others: those who were friends or foes, customers or competitors. So, as soon as WikiLeaks speaks, people listen—and listen intently.

The general idea behind WikiLeaks—exposing once-secret information—and the consequences of doing so are not new. People have placed importance on sharing high-level secrets for a millennium and a half. WikiLeaks is now part of a long history of whistle-blowing—and this history includes the technology information leakers use and the laws that support their existence.

The Birth of Qui Tam

Whistleblowers International, a collection of attorneys and investigators who represent whistle-blowers in legal cases, says the first written mention of the importance of whistle-blowing dates to the year 695 CE. King Wihtred of Kent, in England, declared, "If a freeman works during [the Sabbath], he shall forfeit his [profits], and the man who informs against him shall have half the fine, and [the profits] of the labor." In other words, by law, tattletales were due a monetary reward. More specifically and more importantly, people who reported a violation of their country's legislation—in this case, someone working on a state-decreed holiday—would be paid. With the king's royal decree, the government started encouraging citizens to help uphold the law.

From this 695 law came the Latin term "qui tam." It is shortened from the phrase "*qui tam pro domino rege quam pro se ipso in hac parte sequitur.*" This means "he who prosecutes for himself as well as for the King." To put it in more modern language, someone who brings a qui tam case or lawsuit is a whistle-blower.

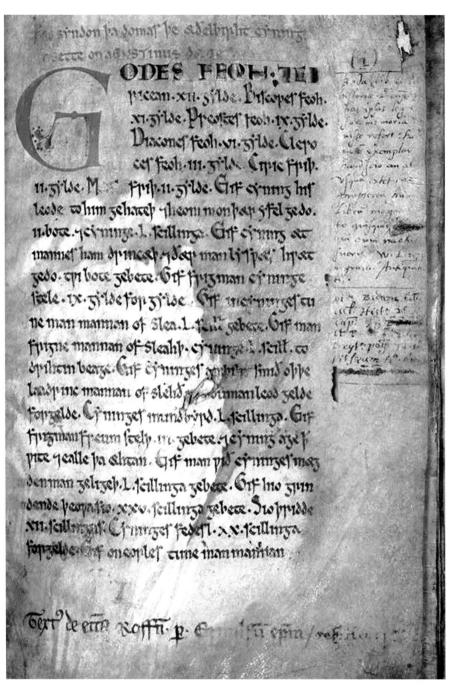

This document contains the oldest remaining copy of King Wihtred's law.

The idea of qui tam was an early import to the United States, arriving when the country was new, and took firm root there. Laws involving qui tam protected and even rewarded private citizens who reported wrongdoings that hurt the country. It didn't matter if these people also became whistle-blowers for their own personal gain. There was no judgment placed on motive. It didn't matter if they were acting wholly selflessly or not. If the information they provided helped the greater good, they were protected. In the eighteenth century, many US state legislatures adopted qui tam provisions.

The False Claims Act

Qui tam lawsuits are now brought under the False Claims Act (FCA). Under this federal legislation, a private citizen may sue a person or business that is defrauding the government. The act not only protects the person—preventing them from being fired, for example—but rewards whistle-blowers. If a qui tam lawsuit recovers government funds, the citizen who brought the suit receives, as payment, some of that recovered money.

Congress passed the FCA on March 2, 1863, in response to fraud against both the Union and the Confederate sides of the Civil War. According to Whistleblowers International, the FCA's sponsor, Senator Jacob Howard, believed that paying whistle-blowers, "even if they had engaged in the corrupt acts themselves," was the "best way to extensively uncover the largest fraudulent schemes." Just as the medieval English qui tam laws met with such success that other countries adopted the law, the FCA has been so useful in the United States that it remains in effect today.

This doesn't mean that the FCA has always been popularly received by the courts. During World War II, US Attorney General Francis Biddle viewed qui tam lawsuits as "opportunistic" and "parasitic," according to Whistleblowers International. He asked the Supreme Court to eliminate the reward offered to whistle-blowers and then asked Congress to abolish the FCA. Perhaps a younger, less robust US government of decades before needed help from citizens, but now Biddle saw the Department of Justice as being fully capable of handling corruption issues. Neither the Supreme Court nor Congress complied with his demands. He did succeed in greatly lessening the number of qui tam cases allowed to come through.

Since World War II, perception has shifted again and the FCA is popular once more. In fact, the year 2015 was its most successful. This resurgence started in the 1980s.

The 1986 False Claim Act Amendments

The 1980s in the United States saw renewed social unrest paired with less government oversight and the farthest-reaching media coverage to date. In this perfect storm, it was the best time for the FCA to be useful again.

Citizens and government alike wanted a strengthened military. Because of this demand, there was room for people to act opportunistically and to take advantage. Corporations started overcharging the US military for supplies, and the military was paying. In the void of very little government oversight, journalists stepped in to monitor the abuse. Their work uncovered things like invoices for $7,622 coffee makers and $435 hammers. By the mid-1980s, four defense contractors had been convicted of fraud.

Seeing the usefulness of the FCA, Congress amended the act in 1986, increasing both the penalties against companies and the rewards for individual whistle-blowers. With this protection, the hope was that employees of defense contractors would step forward sooner with confidential information.

IRS Whistleblower Office

The Internal Revenue Service (IRS), the government department that collects taxes, estimates that tax fraud and evasion by large corporations costs the government $345 billion annually. To address this massive problem, in 2007, the IRS Whistleblower Office opened.

This office has recovered billions of dollars already and attracted some high-profile whistle-blowers. Bradley Birkenfeld was one. He is known for receiving both a steep punishment and a big reward for his efforts.

Birkenfeld had been a banker with UBS, a Swiss bank. While working there, he was asked to illegally hide millions of dollars for American clients. For his role helping these people dodge paying taxes, Birkenfeld went to US federal prison for two and a half years. For his whistle-blowing on the whole operation, he received $104 million from the US government.

Because of his information leak, not only did he receive financial compensation, but so did the US federal government. UBS was forced to pay a multimillion-dollar penalty. Other banks' wrongdoing was discovered during the investigation, and they too have been fined, with at least one being charged a multibillion-dollar penalty. Birkenfeld's whistle-blowing also led to new laws for American money held in foreign banks.

But as of a 2015 interview with CNBC, Birkenfeld didn't think the US government had done enough in response to what they learned from his leak. Relatively few people have been prosecuted for their crimes. Birkenfeld's payout was calculated based on only UBS's penalty; his lawyers argued that he should be rewarded 15 to 30 percent—the percentage allowed by the IRS whistle-blower program—of the total money the IRS will receive from all the wrongdoers. If Birkenfeld hadn't brought USB's crimes to light, the government would never have found the other banks' issues, so it seems logical he would get part of that money too.

The Dodd-Frank Act

The Dodd-Frank Wall Street Reform and Consumer Protection Act of 2010 passed in response to the American financial crisis that began in 2007 and ended in 2009. This era, which would be called the Great Recession, started with a housing crisis involving poorly handled mortgages and the resulting foreclosures. This spiraled to affect other markets. The Dodd-Frank act overhauled Wall Street regulations. Included was the creation of the Securities and Exchange Commissions Office of the Whistleblower (SEC). Like the IRS programs for tax whistle-blowers and the FCA for many other types of informants, the SEC offers punishment and reward regarding investment crimes.

Dodd-Frank has been so successful that the government is considering similar acts to cover whistle-blowers in other industries. Whistleblowers International thinks such legislation could have prevented the 2010 oil spill in the Gulf of Mexico or the 2015 Volkswagen emissions scandal, during which the German car manufacturer admitted to trying to cheat US emissions tests.

Benjamin Franklin: Statesman, Inventor ... and Whistle-Blower

Laws supporting whistle-blowing stretch back to colonial times. It seems even well-respected leaders, such as Benjamin Franklin, saw the benefit in exposing crucial backroom dealings.

In 1773, the Colonies were still trying to become the United States, but stability was difficult to achieve when everyone was so on edge regarding relations with Great Britain. The people of Massachusetts, in particular, were upset because more and more British troops were showing up in their towns. They didn't know why the country they were so desperate to separate from was making threatening moves.

Franklin wanted to calm the people, so he exposed confidential letters about Massachusetts governor Thomas Hutchinson. Hutchinson had been appointed by Britain, and the letters showed his loyalty to the Crown: he had intentionally misled Britain into believing more military presence was needed in Massachusetts. After the letters were leaked, Hutchinson was dishonorably discharged from being governor and went into exile.

Julius Chambers and Nellie Bly

There are lots of reasons why people aren't sure if WikiLeaks should be classified a whistle-blower organization or a media

Benjamin Franklin was responsible for leaked documents.

In 1872, journalist Julius Chambers investigated patient abuse at a hospital.

outlet (or something else entirely). One of the reasons is because the line between whistle-blowing and journalism has always been blurred. Take, for example, Julius Chambers, one of America's first investigative journalists, and one of the biggest stories of his career.

In the late 1800s, there were rumblings that patients were being abused at Bloomingdale Insane Asylum in New York. Chambers pretended to need psychiatric help and checked himself in to the hospital. With evidence he gathered during his stay there, he published revealing articles in the *New York Tribune*. The results were astounding: twelve patients who weren't sick to begin with were released from Bloomingdale. Laws regarding admittance to mental institutions in New

Nellie Bly's *Ten Days in the Madhouse* made her a famous journalist.

York were amended to try to prevent healthy people from being institutionalized. Fifteen years later, journalist Nellie Bly followed in Chambers's footsteps.

Bly checked herself into Blackwell's, an institution in New York City. The articles, and then book, that came out of her investigation not only led to psychiatric hospital reform, but also launched Bly's impressive writing career.

George Custer

George Custer, a famous military commander during the American Civil War and the Indian Wars, was also a whistle-blower.

George Custer may have helped reveal secrets about a US president.

In 1876, during Reconstruction after the American Civil War, Custer learned an ugly secret about US Secretary of War William Belknap. During the war, Belknap had received kickbacks, or money, from a weapons trade he knew was deadly for his soldiers. The guns were faulty.

Rumor has it that Custer was involved in the publishing of an anonymously written *New York Herald* article. The article named names, pointing fingers at people involved in the bad deal, including family members of President Ulysses S. Grant.

Belknap was impeached. Grant, angry and embarrassed, removed Custer from his position of command.

Stewart Menzies

After World War II, Stewart Menzies served as the head of MI6, Britain's foreign intelligence agency, similar to America's CIA. Years before he received that honor and responsibility, Menzies was a common soldier in the British military who witnessed serious wrongdoings.

Menzies saw Intelligence Chief Brigadier John Charteris lie about intelligence estimates. This was in 1917. World War I was still raging and deception could put soldiers' and civilians' lives in danger. Menzies quietly wrote and delivered a report about this to his commanders.

In response, Charteris was removed from his post. Menzies was promoted to the rank of major and, of course, his work was recognized later during his career move up through MI6.

Pentagon Papers

The Pentagon Papers detailed US involvement in Southeast Asia from World War II until May 1968. They were officially titled "Report of the Office of the Secretary of Defense Vietnam Task Force" because US Secretary of Defense

Secretary of Defense Robert McNamara commissioned the project that would become the Pentagon Papers.

Robert McNamara commissioned the project. All of them were labeled as top secret. They were from the US Department of Defense, the US State Department, and the Central Intelligence Agency (CIA). They totaled three thousand pages of narrative, or written story, with four thousand pages of supporting documents. When they were bound together, they formed forty-seven books. Daniel Ellsberg, a senior research associate, participated in the eighteen-monthlong program compiling the documents for McNamara.

Ellsberg was a career military and government man. He had served as a US Marine Corps officer and worked for the Department of Defense. He had supported American action overseas. On the surface, he should not have turned into a whistle-blower against the American military and government. What he read in the Pentagon Papers as he worked on them began to change his mind.

The Pentagon Papers revealed, among other things, a lot about what happened behind the scenes leading to US involvement in the Vietnam War. Presidents Harry Truman, Dwight Eisenhower, and John Kennedy had all made decisions that directly led the country to war—and the American public was kept in the dark about all of that. President Lyndon Johnson began laying the groundwork for war in 1964, a full year before the public was told. In 1965, Johnson ordered the bombing of North Vietnam, which turned out to be not in line with his advisers, but rather against the judgment of the US intelligence community. When Ellsberg learned about how the United States had gotten involved in Southeast Asia, it supported his growing belief that the US military shouldn't be in Vietnam.

Ellsberg felt he couldn't be complicit in keeping these secrets. He secretly photocopied sections and took them to members of Congress. No one responded to his requests

Cablegate Infographic

On November 28, 2010, WikiLeaks began releasing a massive number of top-secret US documents in what would come to be known as Cablegate. Germany's *Spiegel*, one of the media outlets that received access to the documents, called the leak "no less than a political meltdown for American foreign policy."

To help readers understand the data, many media outlets created interactive images and infographics about the cables and their content. The *Guardian*'s map and corresponding images showed how many cables were sent from each city, and how many of those were categorized "confidential" versus "secret" versus "unclassified." The infographic also includes the years of the earliest cables, some of which were from as early as the 1960s. Most were from after 2000.

Every cable was tagged with its subject or subjects. The most common of these were listed in the *Guardian* infographic's keyword section. For example, diplomatic messages labeled with "PREL" talked about external political relations; those listed as "ECON" discussed economic conditions; and "PTER" cables focused on terrorism.

The WikiLeaks cables

A look at the 251,287 U.S. embassy cables leaked recently:

Few cables secret

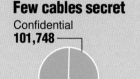

Confidential
101,748

Unclassified
133,887

Secret
15,652

- **Time frame** Oldest cable from 1966; newest, February 2010; most written in the past few years

- **Top subjects discussed**

External political relations

Internal governmental affairs

Human rights

Economic conditions

Terrorists, terrorism

Source: WikiLeaks

Cable origin, top sources

■ **Secret** ■ **Confidential** **Unclassified**

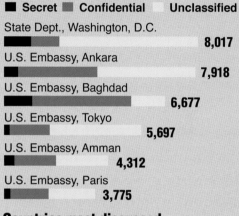

State Dept., Washington, D.C.
8,017

U.S. Embassy, Ankara
7,918

U.S. Embassy, Baghdad
6,677

U.S. Embassy, Tokyo
5,697

U.S. Embassy, Amman
4,312

U.S. Embassy, Paris
3,775

Countries most discussed

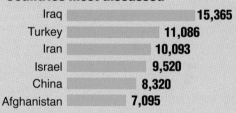

Iraq **15,365**

Turkey **11,086**

Iran **10,093**

Israel **9,520**

China **8,320**

Afghanistan **7,095**

Graphic: Judy Treible

© 2010 MCT

for an investigation, so Ellsberg turned to the media. He leaked major sections of the Pentagon Papers to the *New York Times* and the *Washington Post.* On June 13, 1971, the *New York Times* began publishing a series of articles about them.

The government responded immediately, and by the third day of reporting, the US Department of Justice had obtained a temporary restraining order against further publication of the classified documents. The government cited "immediate and irreparable harm" to US national defense if the newspaper continued to publish. The newspapers had to stop writing about the documents immediately.

They didn't just give up. For more than two weeks, the two newspapers fought the order, and on June 30, 1971, they won. The US Supreme Court ruled in *New York Times Co. v. United States* that the government's argument wasn't strong enough. There was no proof of harm to national security, and publishing the papers was permissible under the First Amendment, which includes freedom of the press. In a 6–3 decision—meaning six justices voted in favor of the newspapers' right to publish and three voted that they did not have that right—the court allowed the press to resume publishing the material. This has become known as a landmark case, a case that sets a precedent for others, a case that lawyers cite to win arguments and that judges rely on to make sound rulings in similar matters.

The public was ready for information similar to these documents. People had been growing tired of the war and suspicious of the government's justifications for it. The Pentagon Papers offered proof that the United States had

(*above*) Daniel Ellsberg surrenders to authorities at the Boston Federal Building.

(*left*) Thieves looked for damaging information about Daniel Ellsberg in his psychiatrist's locked cabinet.

gone to war foolishly and recklessly. They helped the American public demand better of their government and military.

President Richard Nixon's administration indicted Ellsberg on criminal charges, including conspiracy, espionage, and stealing government property. The White House even hired people to break into Ellsberg's psychiatrist's office to read his files, looking for information that would discredit him. When that activity came to light, the trial against Ellsberg was dismissed.

Though the right to publish the documents was won, the full Pentagon Papers weren't declassified and released until June of 2011, "36 to 40 years overdue," Ellsberg wrote in an opinion piece for the *Guardian*. But he saw the release as unfortunately timely, because the United States was "mired again in wars—especially in Afghanistan—remarkably similar to the 30-year conflict in Vietnam," he wrote.

He wished that the American people, beyond learning from history (which the Pentagon Papers provide), could learn from then-current affairs with "the Pentagon Papers of Iraq and Afghanistan (and Pakistan, Yemen and Libya)." He called on investigative journalist Bob Woodward, who published a book in 2010 on President Barack Obama and the war in Afghanistan, as well as his sources, to give WikiLeaks the documentation behind what they said in the book. Ellsberg wanted WikiLeaks to get the information because he has been impressed with their ability to share information with the public quickly.

In 2010, WikiLeaks released ninety thousand documents regarding the United States's involvement in Afghanistan.

The leak was called the biggest since the Pentagon Papers, an impressive comparison.

Frank Serpico

Frank Serpico was a New York City police officer in the 1960s and 1970s. He testified before the Knapp Commission,

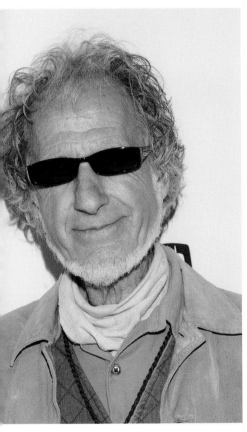

Frank Serpico poses for a photo in 2017.

a panel that was studying corruption within the police department. By doing so, Serpico became the first police officer to testify against other officers. This is a big deal: loyalty is everything in groups like the police force, where the members place themselves in danger regularly and must know they can completely trust their fellow officers.

On one hand, what Serpico did changed policing forever, for the better. He stood up to a system that was allowing cops to take bribes for looking the other way when crimes happened. On the other hand, he showed he didn't have his colleagues' backs unconditionally. "Police make up a peculiar subculture in society," Serpico wrote years later. "More often than not

Karen Silkwood risked a lot to expose corporate secrets.

they have their own moral code of behavior, an 'us against them' attitude, enforced by a Blue Wall of Silence."The Blue Wall refers to the blue uniforms cops wear. "Speak out, and you're no longer 'one of us.' You're one of 'them.'" Serpico paid a price for his outspokenness. During a drug raid after he testified, he was shot, and the other police officers refused to help him. He survived, though he became deaf in one ear and would forever walk with a limp.

Karen Silkwood

Karen Silkwood was born in 1946 in Longview, Texas. For twenty-six of what would be only twenty-eight years of life, Karen lived quietly and privately. She dropped out of college, where she had been studying science, and got married. When she divorced, she moved to Oklahoma City, headquarters for Kerr-McGee Corporation's oil and nuclear complex, and landed a job at its plutonium plant.

Karen was open-minded about the company's research, but as soon as she understood better the extreme hazards of plutonium, she became concerned that management wasn't being careful in its handling of the substance. She thought the Kerr-McGee plant was "sloppy, dishonest and unsafe," wrote the author of a *Rolling Stone* article on her whistle-blowing. She didn't just worry privately—she spoke out. While her coworkers applauded her courage, even electing her to the local steering committee of the Oil, Chemical and Atomic Workers International Union, the higher-ups were not as interested in hearing her perspective.

The leadership rung of Kerr-McGee had been some of the most powerful people in the country for a while by then.

The company's founder, Robert Kerr, had been governor of Oklahoma, ran for president as a Democrat in 1952, and at the time of his death in 1963, was a powerful Senator. Dean McGee, Kerr's successor in the company, advised President Kennedy on defense policies and President Gerald Ford on energy.

With her union's encouragement, Karen began working undercover to gather company files. Soon, she felt she had enough documents of interest, and she set a meeting with a reporter from the *New York Times*. She gathered the documents and got in her Honda. She didn't make it to the meeting. Her car hit a concrete wall and swerved off the road. The reason why was murky. Her autopsy showed alcohol and prescription sedatives in her system, which may have caused her to fall asleep at the wheel. It also showed that she had been exposed to large amounts of radiation. Not only did she work near radioactivity, of course, but plutonium contamination had been found in her apartment as well: in her bathroom, and oddly, in a bologna-and-cheese sandwich in her refrigerator. Kerr-McGee lawyers suggested she'd poisoned herself. Those who knew her of course argued against that. In addition, a private investigator found evidence she could have been pushed off the road. The highway patrolman who helped at the scene of the accident said he'd picked up documents that had scattered across the highway and put them back in Karen's car. Those were the ones Karen had taken from work and was planning to leak to the *New York Times*. When Karen's friends claimed her car the next day, the documents were gone.

Karen's death ended up being another beginning in the story. Her death, the mysteriousness of it, and what it revealed of her undercover work, kicked off a whole new layer to the investigation. It even led to another young woman, journalist Jacque Srouji, working undercover, obtaining secret documents, and coming up against a huge, powerful force trying to stop her.

Franklin v. Parke-Davis

Until 1987, most lawsuits that were filed under the whistle-blowers' protection legislation had to do with the military. Since 1987, over half have dealt with the health care industry—uncovering everything from overbilling to the payment of kickbacks.

Franklin v. Parke-Davis (1996) was a major turning point for whistle-blowing in the health-care industry. It set a precedent for future cases. The Franklin in the case's name was whistle-blower Dr. David Franklin. He had worked for the pharmaceutical company Parke-Davis and was concerned about its off-label promotion of one of its drugs.

If a drug is approved by the FDA to treat one condition, but the pharmaceutical company markets the drug as being able to treat other illnesses as well, that is off-label promoting. Franklin's attorney argued that this fraud caused false medical claims to be submitted to the government, thereby costing the government money it shouldn't have spent. This was a new, unproven argument, and the government declined to get involved, as it usually did for FCA lawsuits.

Franklin and his attorney persisted anyway and won, changing how the government considers such suits. By now,

David Franklin's case was important to health care.

off-label FCA lawsuits have recovered nearly eight billion dollars for the government. Franklin's whistle-blowing affected the promotion of not only the drug he was most concerned about, but the marketing of many drugs to come.

Technology to Leak

Laws supportive of leaking and publishing once-secret information help to create an atmosphere in which whistle-blowers, like Assange and those who publish through his WikiLeaks site, are expected and, at least to a degree, accepted. Individuals who have leaked information in the past help to inspire whistle-blowers of today. Advancements in technology are a third piece to the historical background behind Assange and WikiLeaks. On a basic level, WikiLeaks couldn't exist without computers. It also couldn't exist without technology such as anonymizing practices.

Ctunnel, a service to make communication on the internet anonymous, was one such effort setting the stage for WikiLeaks' existence. Penet also anonymized user information. Created by hacker Johan Helsingius in the mid-1990s, it stripped emails of their senders' true information before sending the information along.

There also had to be systems in place on which hackers, who become whistle-blowers if they release the information they find on a computer network, could communicate electronically. By 1993, Assange was in charge of one such system, Suburbia Public Access Network. It was one of Australia's first internet service providers (ISPs). Assange has said that Suburbia served as "one of the biggest prototypes for WikiLeaks." Through it, activists could share information.

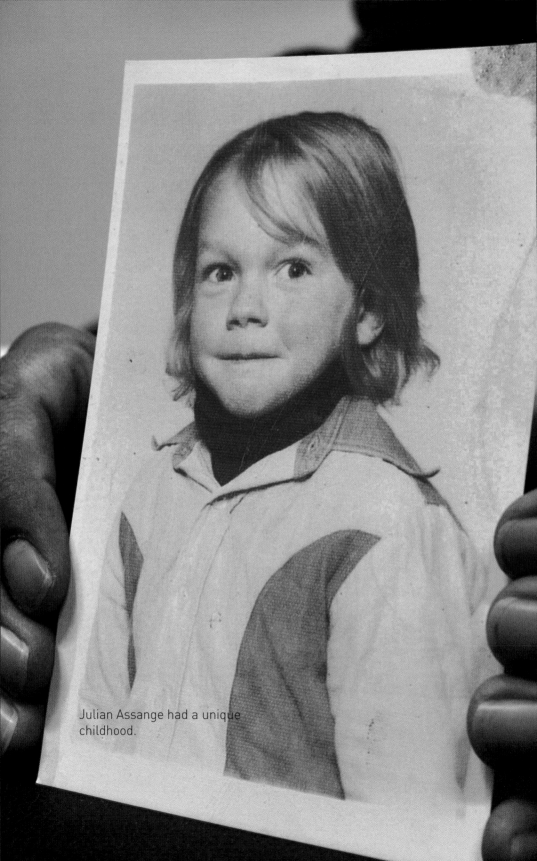

Julian Assange had a unique childhood.

A Brief History of
Julian Assange
and WikiLeaks

When Christine Hawkins was seventeen years old, she burned her schoolbooks and hopped on a motorcycle, heading by herself across her homeland of Australia to the island nation's most populous city, Sydney. By her early twenties, she had moved on again, to the tiny coastal town of Townsville. There, on July 3, 1971, she gave birth to her son, Julian Paul Hawkins.

A Legacy of Being Unconventional

Julian's birth father, John Shipton, wasn't in the picture much. Court documents released decades later, in 2011, list Shipton as the nominal owner of WikiLeaks.org. By the time Julian was one year old, a theater director named Brett Assange had married

Christine and given Julian his last name. According to the *Mail & Guardian* newspaper, Assange has talked about his father a few times, although it's always unclear which man he's referring to. Still, as much as his mother's worldview would influence Assange, so too does he credit male family members for his opinions: "Men don't create victims. They try to stop people from becoming victims," he has said, describing this "value [of mine] that comes from my father."

The family lived for part of Assange's childhood on Magnetic Island off the Australian coast, which had a population of five hundred, though the number fluctuated. The *Sydney Morning Herald* reported that most of those residents were "highly transient," moving around a lot, just like Assange's family.

"Most of this period of my childhood was pretty Tom Sawyer," Assange told the *New Yorker*, likening himself to the fictional Mark Twain character who played and explored along the Mississippi River. The rent on their first house was twelve dollars a week; their second house, on an abandoned pineapple farm, required them to bushwhack their way to the front door with a machete.

When Assange was eight years old, his mother and Brett Assange divorced. His mother began dating another man, with whom she had another son, Assange's half-brother. Their relationship was never very happy; the anger escalated into something scary, and Christine and the kids went on the run for five years until Assange was sixteen. They hid from Christine's ex-boyfriend, who continued to try to find them.

Part of the reason the boyfriend was so dangerous was that he belonged to a powerful Australian doomsday cult,

Julian Assange spent part of his childhood on Magnetic Island, Australia.

the Family. Leader Anne Hamilton-Byrne called herself the reincarnation of Jesus and gathered followers in the 1960s. She didn't look for adults only to join her, but children as well, whom she beat, starved, drugged, and tortured emotionally. Assange's mother may have feared her ex-boyfriend would "give" her children to the cult. The boyfriend, Assange told the *Guardian* newspaper decades later, had been "a sinister presence" who sought to have "a certain psychological power" over his family, just as Hamilton-Byrne would have demanded of him. As an adult, Assange reflected on his years hiding from the boyfriend as a terrifying game of cat and mouse. He suspected the Family had moles in the government who provided the man with leads on where Assange and his mother and half-brother were. This kind of watchfulness, or paranoia, has also served Assange as an adult, being aware of who's tracking him as he tells some of the world's biggest secrets.

Assange followed in his mother's footsteps when it came to starting a family. As she had, he did so at a young age. At sixteen, he fell in love, and at eighteen, his girlfriend became pregnant. They got married and their child, a son named Daniel, was born soon afterward.

Two years later, his wife had left him, taking their toddler with her. For eight years, Assange fought for custody, sometimes claiming his wife's new home was unsafe for their son. His mother had never been fond of human-created systems (she even kept her kids out of the education system), and she called the state during her son's fight over his child "a great bureaucracy that was squashing people." With her son and another activist, she formed an organization called Parent Inquiry Into Child Protection.

"We used full-on activist methods," Christine told the *New Yorker*. They secretly recorded conversations with officials. Using the Australian Freedom of Information Act, they obtained relevant documents. They encouraged child-protection workers to leak inside information. This was one of Assange's earliest connections to whistle-blowing.

In 1999, Assange and his ex-wife reached a custody agreement. Since then, Assange has had several more children. Because his private life is under constant public scrutiny, they live under assumed names.

A Unique Education

Assange's young childhood was highly adventurous—riding horses, building rafts, fishing, and clamoring around old mine shafts and tunnels, as he told the *New Yorker*—but it was not like that simply because he lived for a while on a tiny island. It was also because his family moved thirty-seven times by the time he was fourteen.

In part because of that physical instability and in part because of his mother's distrust of formal education, Assange never went to school. He was homeschooled, took correspondence courses, and met informally with college professors whenever he moved to a place where he could. Eventually, as a young adult, Assange enrolled in traditional school, the University of Melbourne, in Australia. He studied physics, but he didn't find the intellectual stimulation he sought in either the subject or his fellow students.

Libraries were one of his biggest teachers. "I spent a lot of time in libraries going from one thing to another, looking closely at the books I found in citations, and followed that trail," Assange told the *New Yorker*. Because of the way he taught himself, reading voraciously and silently, he grew his vocabulary but he couldn't practice pronunciation. He learned how to pronounce a lot of the words much later.

As a young teen, he lived across the street from an electronics store. He took advantage of this by spending time in the store writing computer code on a Commodore 64, one of the earliest home computers, first produced in 1982. His mother was his biggest cheerleader; she felt nothing but respect for how "highly intelligent" her son was, even wondering at one point if he was "too smart for himself," the *Swedish Wire* reported in 2010. Eventually, his mother moved them to a cheaper home so she could afford to buy him the computer. "Julian had been drooling over these things [computers] for about a year and I just thought that he really needed to have it for his intellectual growth," Christine told the *Sydney Morning Herald*. The computer cost $600 Australian ($400 in US dollars).

Assange Makes a Lifelong Friend: Computers

Assange has likened working with computers to playing chess: both are austere activities, stripped down but strict and harsh in their simplicity. Both "don't have many rules, there is no randomness, and the problem is very hard," he told the *New Yorker*.

Julian Assange had an early personal computer.

Getting that Commodore 64 under his own roof was the start of something very big for thirteen-year-old Assange. It was the start, really, of everything for him. In 1987, when he was sixteen, he added a modem to his home setup. Though there was no internet to connect to, there were enough sufficiently linked networks and systems to form a different "hidden electronic landscape," the *New Yorker* explained.

Programmers, like Assange was becoming, could hack into different networks and make their electronic presence known there. Once again, Assange was running independently through the wilds. As a young child, his playground was the tiny, rocky Magnetic Island; now, as a slightly older child, he was poking around in networks including those belonging to the US Department of Defense and the Los Alamos National Laboratory. These organizations study and solve issues of American national security. Later, a lead Australian investigator working against Assange said of the young hacker, "I think he acted on the belief that everyone should have access to everything."

Along with two others, Assange formed the International Subversives. He said they followed hackers' golden rules of not damaging or altering the systems they broke into. Still, one day, the police raided the teenager's one-machine home computer lab. Someone had alleged that he'd stolen $500,000 from a bank. He was never charged, and his equipment was returned, but now the International Subversives were solidly on the authorities' radar. The federal police even set up Operation Weather to keep tabs on the three members.

Knowing this nearly destroyed Assange. He told the *New Yorker* that he hardly slept, dreaming "of footsteps crunching on the driveway gravel, of shadows in the pre-dawn darkness, of a gun-toting police squad bursting through his back door at 5:00 a.m." In the early 1990s, there still was no internet to speak of, no cloud, not even thumb drives. There were disks: big, square physical disks that even expert hackers had to deal with. Assange started hiding his computer disks in an apiary he kept, hoping no one would think to search for them among buzzing, swarming bees.

On October 29, 1991, Assange's nightmares came true. The police arrived at his door and charged him with thirty-one counts of computer-related crimes, including hacking. As much as they were trying to punish him, they were also trying to use him as an example. The lead Operation Weather investigator told the *New Yorker* that the government's directive was that they "establish a deterrent" for future

Julian Assange was a teenage genius with computers.

hackers. Computer crimes were a brand-new police focus, and they wanted to stop criminals before they started.

Assange survived the three-year-long case, though it wasn't mentally easy on him. In the end, the judge agreed with the young hacker that he had acted purely with the purpose of "intelligent inquisitiveness and the pleasure of being able to." There was no real wrongdoing, and he was free.

The Birth of WikiLeaks

In 2006, Assange began frenzied construction of WikiLeaks in a house outside of the University of Melbourne. He created an ad hoc team to help him, inviting travelers passing through the university to stay with him. They diagrammed plans for the future WikiLeaks on his home's walls and doors.

His manifesto, "Conspiracy as Governance," applied graph theory to politics. Assange argued that cutting off communication within a bureaucratic body was the key to killing it. A disruption in a government's lines of internal communication would affect the rate of information flow. Once the information ceased to be exchanged among members of the government, the conspiracy of government would be gone. The way to disrupt communication was as simple and as difficult as playing chess and programming computers: "Leaks," the *New Yorker* wrote in its profile of Assange, "were an instrument of information warfare."

CNET's 2017 "What Is WikiLeaks?" is a good up-to-date Q&A on what Assange grew. At eleven years old, WikiLeaks, an international nonprofit with more than one hundred staff members, has published more than ten

Julian Assange
smiles for a
snapshot.

million documents. Some are previously classified original documents, and some are reports of analyses explaining the information and putting it in context. WikiLeaks is nothing if not savvy about its publicity, so it is known for releasing information in a timely manner. Whenever news about a particular topic will have a big impact on the world, because of other events happening at the same time, that's when WikiLeaks releases the secrets it knows. So far, it has published ten million documents, but it likely has a lot more waiting to be released.

Whistle-blowing is an important part of the Assange-WikiLeaks story, even though they aren't technically whistle-blowers. They distribute or publish information from whistle-blowers. The lines between Assange and WikiLeaks and whistle-blowers can seem blurry. First, the two need each other and work closely together. WikiLeaks relies on whistle-blowers to exist. They are the ones that supply what WikiLeaks publishes. Whistle-blowers don't need WikiLeaks to exist. People have made secret information public for centuries before this organization existed—but the organization has the prestige and the know-how to make sure leaked information gets seen and heard. It currently offers the biggest return impact for a leaker's hard work. The second reason that WikiLeaks seems akin to a whistle-blower is that it protects its sources so fiercely. The actual whistle-blowers are kept anonymous, protecting those people from retaliation by their employers or other groups concerned by the leaks.

The point at which it's clear that WikiLeaks is a publisher and not an informant is when it comes to retaliation. If a source is outed and it comes to light who exactly leaked information, that person can be charged with criminal offenses. It's happened to some of WikiLeaks' sources, like Chelsea Manning, whose story is in another chapter. When someone outside of WikiLeaks told authorities that she had leaked military intelligence, she was charged with espionage and was imprisoned. The US government has threatened to bring similar charges against Assange and WikiLeaks, but experts think they'd have a hard time winning the case because they are technically publishers. They are protected by freedom of the press.

One final, small, but confusing point should be clarified: WikiLeaks and Wikipedia are not related. A wiki, which is part of both of their names, is a website on which multiple people write and edit the same information. Wikipedia, the online encyclopedia, is the most recognizable wiki. Anyone can edit the entries, and visitors to the site can see a history of the edits made, what was changed, by whom, and when. WikiLeaks used to be a wiki and maintains that part of its name because its name is so well-known.

Assange's Personality

Even as a teenager, Assange was very selective about who he spent his time with. He believed he and a friend of his "were bright sensitive kids who didn't fit into the dominant subculture and fiercely castigated those who did as irredeemable boneheads," the *New Yorker* reported. In many news outlets, Assange has attributed his directness at least a little to his childhood in the Australian state of Queensland, "where people spoke their minds bluntly." Assange once told the *New Yorker*: "When you are much brighter than the people you are hanging around with, which I was as a teenager, two things happen. First of all, you develop an enormous ego. Secondly, you start to think that everything can be solved with just a bit of thinking—but ideology is too simple to address how things work."

His attitude did not temper with age and distance from the northeastern coast. As a thirty-five-year-old in the city of Melbourne, along the country's southeastern coast, he had equally stern words for nine hundred physicists. They were attendees of a conference organized by the Australian Institute of Physics, and, according to a blog post by Assange, they were "sniveling fearful conformists of woefully, woefully inferior character."

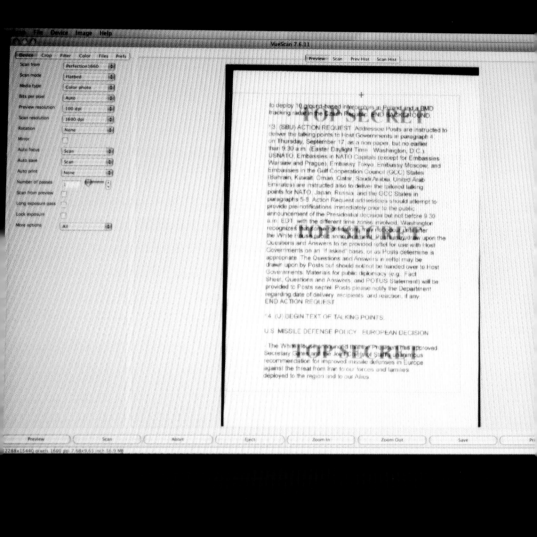

With computers, top secret documents can quickly become public.

The "Ordinary" People in WikiLeaks' Leaks

With every document that WikiLeaks releases, people
lose their anonymity—their names and details of their
lives are shared with the public. Because WikiLeaks
releases government and corporate papers, the lives
of ordinary citizens aren't always revealed. Many of
the people mentioned lead somewhat public lives and
can't be expected to be totally unknown. Still, they
aren't always widely known—the president of the United
States is known by everyone, but most of the world
doesn't know about a diplomat from Turkey, for example.
Certainly, their family and friends are private people, but
they too can be caught up in leaked documents. They are
very much affected by WikiLeaks, but in the shadow cast
by the more serious details the documents reveal. The
way their world has changed can be forgotten.

During Cablegate in 2010, WikiLeaks sent select
media outlets about a quarter of a million messages
from the US State Department and US embassies
around the world. Then, journalists had to decide how
much to share with their audiences. The *New York Times*
said it removed some names and passages from the

documents it published, replacing particularly sensitive details with "XXXXXXXXXXXX." Still, a lot of names and details remained.

In the story of "A Wild Wedding in Dagestan, Russia," one of the documents released during Cablegate, the newspaper used the short row of X's only four times. All the other details of a lavish three-day wedding in 2006, which an American diplomat attended, remained. These details included names of some of the guests. Maybe over coffee or on their way to work, American readers of the *Times* learned that the father of the groom, an oil tycoon, offered his summer estate for some of the wedding's festivities. The property included access to the Caspian Sea and a forty-meter (44-yard) airport tower. Yes, the groom's family was well-known in their region because of their wealth, but until this leak, most Americans had no idea they existed. Suddenly, they were akin to reality television personalities, at least for a few pages of a once-classified and now-public report.

The Dagestan region in southern Russia is volatile, with most of the still-living city leaders only still living because they have survived assassination attempts. The diplomat wrote that the father of the groom "gave us a lift in the Rolls once in Moscow, but the legroom was somewhat constricted by the presence of a Kalashnikov carbine at our feet." The estate was also heavily fortified.

The entertainment at the wedding included never-ending dishes of fine foods prepared on-site by chefs, thousands of bottles of vodka specially flown in, performances by local bands and international pop stars, fireworks, and even a performer known as the Accordion King. During the dancing, guests showered those on the dance floor with American hundred-dollar bills.

Not only could *New York Times* readers glimpse through this document—once marked confidential and now publicly displayed—social customs of a faraway land, but they learned about "the deadly serious North Caucasus politics of land, ethnicity, clan, and alliance" that underlay everything. The document's final section was all about "the practical uses of a Caucasus wedding," meaning that politics, power, and diplomacy were as much the reason for a wedding as was love, maybe even more. At one point, a colonel in Russia's state security organization, the FSB, sat down next to the American diplomat who filed the report. Very drunk, he started lightly harassing the American group. "We were inclined to cut the Colonel some slack, though: he is head of the unit to combat terrorism in Dagestan ... extremists have sooner or later assassinated everyone who has joined that unit."

Assange's work has taught people about much behind-the-scenes minutia that could have major effects on a region or the world.

Assange wasn't always outwardly dismissive of those he felt he'd bested. In September of 1991, during his early days of hacking, he broke in to the master terminal at Nortel. Nortel was a Canadian telecom company, maintained in Melbourne. A company administrator was also in the system, which meant Assange was about to be found out, he later told the *New Yorker*. So, Assange made a joke. "For years, I have been struggling in this grayness. But now I have finally seen the light." He then politely asked the administrator not to call the police as he backed away without doing harm.

His treatment of others did not go unnoticed. As the *Mail & Guardian* reported, one of Assange's defense attorneys testified, "He was ostracized from time to time ... He would be bullied and his only real savior in life or his own bedrock in life was this computer."

While awaiting trial in the early 1990s, he became so depressed that he even checked himself into a hospital. After being discharged, he moved into the dense eucalyptus forests of Dandenong Ranges National Park in Victoria, Australia. There, he had no one to choose or reject as his friend but himself. "Your inner voice quiets down," he told the *New Yorker*. "Your vision of yourself disappears."

Assange grew up in a household suspicious of convention of all kinds. When Operation Weather brought him to trial, for what he saw as a victimless crime of just looking around inside corporate and government computer networks, his mind was ready to accept a certain outlook on the situation. The *New Yorker* explained, "He had come to understand the defining human struggle ... as individual versus institution."

Hierarchies and bureaucracies were at odds with and ultimately destroyed truth, creativity, love, and compassion.

As he waited for that first trial to end, he read Aleksandr Solzhenitsyn's *The First Circle* not once, but three times. This was a novel about scientists and technicians forced into the Gulag, the Soviet Union's forced-labor prison camp. "How close the parallels to my own adventures!" he wrote. He may like to draw connections between his life and the lives of a diverse array of people. For example, during Assange's 2017 interview with the *New Yorker*, a friend of his visited and brought with him a gift: *Debriefing the President: The Interrogation of Saddam Hussein*, by a former CIA agent who believed the Iraqi leader had been misunderstood. "I know you'll love it," the friend told Assange, perhaps because he would see similarities in the ways he may be misunderstood. In other words, the *New Yorker* reporter suggested, Assange can be considered "someone with a romantic view of himself in the world … who is also titanically self-absorbed."

Julian Assange speaks
to the press.

Chapter Four

Hero, Villain, or Somewhere in Between?

A ctivist, hacker, publisher, whistle-blower, hero, criminal; intelligent, paranoid, tragic, truth-seeker. All these words, and many more, have been used to describe Julian Assange. As of August 2017, he was five years into also being called "asylum seeker." In a story that is incredibly long and detailed for a person who was only forty-six at the time, it's useful to ground ourselves in Assange's physical time and space. Where Assange was living in asylum, and why, gives us a starting point to consider the question "Is he a hero or a villain?"

Assange in Political Asylum

In June 2012, Assange arrived at the Ecuadorian embassy in London. He was disguised as a motorcycle courier because he needed to travel without attracting the attention of police. He was seeking political asylum. Considering his work as founder and ongoing head of WikiLeaks, an organization responsible for making public huge amounts of classified information, the logical assumption would be that he was seeking protection from a criminal charge related to that. He is, after all, considered both hero and villain for his work with WikiLeaks.

That is why he continued to stay at the embassy. Years later, his concern for his freedom made him a resident of the embassy for the foreseeable future. The reason he first went to the embassy was for controversy within his personal life.

Two years before, in August 2010, Sweden issued an arrest warrant for Assange because two women said he had sexually assaulted them while he was in the country for a conference. Assange denied the accusation, saying he had harmed no one. The next two years were a back and forth of warrants being issued and withdrawn, and Assange going into custody and posting bail. Finally, when orders were given that Assange be extradited to Sweden for trial, he sought asylum, and Ecuador granted it. Assange could stay in that country's embassy in London—basically, a patch of Ecuador within Britain. Authorities from Britain and Sweden weren't allowed in to take him to trial, though they tried.

Britain responded to Ecuador giving Assange asylum by saying it would nullify the embassy's diplomatic protection and enter by force. That didn't worry Ecuadorian officials, and Britain backed down in its threats. Police officers did stand outside Assange's quarters and bang on the walls throughout each night for a while. Assange had his own pair of handcuffs

Julian Assange addresses a crowd from Ecuador's embassy in London.

ready, so, if the British authorities did storm in, he could chain himself to the embassy.

Throughout all this, the women maintained that he had attacked them and made them act against their will. Still, their case slowly fizzled to a close: Sweden dropped the case of one of the women in 2015 because the statute of limitations had expired. In other words, even if Assange had done something wrong, the time limit on the crime was up. He was in the clear because enough time had passed. Authorities continued to investigate the other woman's case, but in May 2017, that was dropped as well. Sweden had run up against a seemingly impassable roadblock: if Assange would never leave the Ecuadorian embassy and if Ecuador would continue its protection of him, Sweden simply couldn't complete the investigation.

This, of course, has marred Assange's reputation. It's hard to label someone a hero if they have hurt another person. But throughout Assange's five-year residency at the embassy in London, he has continued to do his work as WikiLeaks' leader. Many people continue to admire him for that. Many people continue to hate him for that too, separate from any crimes he may have committed in his personal life. In fact, the Ecuadorian government granted him asylum not because of the assault charges, but because Assange also faced extradition to the United States. They were considering charges of espionage because of information Assange's site published. For that reason, Assange chose to stay under Ecuador's protection in London.

In April 2017, US Attorney General Jeff Sessions called arresting Assange a "priority" for the justice department.

During a Senate hearing in May 2017, then-FBI Director James Comey said, "People can argue that maybe there is conduct WikiLeaks has engaged in the past that's closer to regular news gathering but in my view, a huge portion of WikiLeaks' activities has nothing to do with legitimate news gathering."

Assange and WikiLeaks Controversies

WikiLeaks and Assange are involved in so many events that this book needed to narrow the list of points for discussion. The following were pulled from lists of "most interesting WikiLeaks," as suggested by media and WikiLeaks itself.

Chelsea Manning

WikiLeaks is known for making classified documents public. Behind these impersonal, often massive, data dumps are real humans: those who wrote the documents, those who are subjects of the documents, and those who are affected by the documents' release into the public sphere.

Chelsea Manning, a former US Army intelligence analyst, is one individual whose life was drastically changed because of WikiLeaks. Because of one decision that threw her into the spotlight in 2010, twists and turns continue to come her way.

Manning was born in Oklahoma in 1987, but grew up in the country of Wales. Though she lived as a male named Bradley until her twenties, she is a candidate for gender-reassignment surgery and will be referred to with female pronouns throughout this section.

Chelsea Manning leaves an event in 2017.

After secondary school, she joined the US Army. She did so for a variety of reasons, some that she hoped would benefit her personally, but also some that were selfless: she told the *New York Times Magazine* that watching the news reports from Iraq and Afghanistan inspired her to want to make a positive difference for her country and in the world. In October 2009, she was deployed to Iraq; by May of the next year, she was posting Facebook messages that indicated her unhappiness with her role in the military as well as a failed personal relationship. Weeks after that, she was arrested for stealing military secrets and became a household name.

Manning had leaked military documents to WikiLeaks, and, as Assange and his staff pride themselves on doing for their sources, they kept her identity a secret. They weren't the only ones who knew she was behind the leak. A hacker Manning had befriended online turned her in. He gave authorities messages she sent him about what she had done: "Listened and lip-synced to Lady Gaga's 'Telephone' while exfiltrating possibly the largest data spillage in American history," Manning wrote of what she sent to WikiLeaks. "Weak servers, weak logging, weak physical security, weak counterintelligence, inattentive signal analysis … a perfect storm," she wrote regarding gaining access to the information.

Though Manning was a private first class, meaning she ranked low in the military hierarchy and earned very little money, she worked as an intelligence analyst. This gave her daily access to highly sensitive information. She worked the eight-hour overnight shift in a small building, skimming reports from American troops to find the most important information to share with senior-level intelligence officers. After a while, she told the *New York Times Magazine*, "'I stopped seeing records and started seeing people: bloody American soldiers, bullet-ridden Iraqi soldiers." It was like when she'd connected to the human stories of the war through the television news—only now she was positioned to do something about it.

Manning had learned about WikiLeaks when she was in computer security training in 2008, two years before. A few months later, she was logging in to online hacker conversations about the organization. In 2010, an idea took shape in her mind. Right before a two-week leave, she downloaded classified reports from work onto discs she labeled "Lady Gaga." During her vacation in the United States, she made her decision to share the information. She tried to give it to any one of several newspapers, but meetings never happened. Finally, on February 3, 2010, she sent the files to WikiLeaks electronically. Her cover letter said: "This is possibly one of the more significant documents of our time removing the fog of war and revealing the true nature of twenty-first-century asymmetric warfare. Have a good day."

In November 2010, the *New York Times*, London's the *Guardian*, Paris's *Le Monde*, Madrid's *El País*, and Germany's *Der Spiegel* were given copies of these files. They included 243,270 diplomatic cables between US embassies around the world to the US State Department. There were also 8,017 orders from the State Department back out to its diplomatic outposts. *Der Spiegel* wrote of what would become known as Cablegate, "Never before in history has a superpower lost control of such vast amounts of such sensitive information—data that can help paint a picture of the foundation upon which US foreign policy is built."

Like a lot of people the world over, the staff of a British magazine called the *Week* pored over the published messages. It published its own article breaking down the information and sharing some of the key insights revealed, like how the king of Saudi Arabia encouraged the United States to attack Iran; the United States had been secretly bombing Yemen; and China was behind a series of cyberattacks on everyone from Google to the Dalai Lama's personal computer.

Because the messages cover years, taken as a collection, they paint a picture of change over time. For example, George W. Bush, who was president of the United States in 2001–2009, faced a very different situation regarding US military involvement in Tehran, the Iranian capital city, than Barack Obama, president for the eight years following. The *New York Times* said the cables that WikiLeaks released "tell the disparate diplomatic back stories of two administrations." The newspaper also reported that the "traditional boundaries between statesmen and spy" shifted over the years, as evidenced in the cables. It is fascinating to now understand these changes from conversations happening behind-the-scenes.

Time magazine included the "diplo-disses" in its reporting on the release—in other words, the gossip from American officials stationed abroad. For example, in one message, a US official called North Korea's then-ruler Kim Jong Il a "flabby old chap." Silvio Berlusconi, then prime minister of Italy, was "feckless, vain, and ineffective as a modern European leader," another official wrote.

One of the Most Memorable Manning Documents

WikiLeaks released Manning's tens of thousands of pieces of information relating to the Afghan war. More than ninety thousand pieces in total, the leak was called the biggest since Daniel Ellsberg leaked the Pentagon Papers during the Vietnam War. The documents were divided into more than one hundred categories and discussed everything from civilian deaths to the hunt for al-Qaeda's leader, Osama bin Laden. The collection included not just written narratives. It also included video footage of an Apache helicopter killing twelve civilians in Baghdad in 2007.

According to a Reuters article, the organization said it had to break the video's encryption code so it could view and investigate the truthfulness of it. In a second confirmation, a US defense official told Reuters, anonymously, that what the video showed had really happened. Though WikiLeaks says it checks the information it receives before it releases it, it is always up to each media organization to confirm.

In the video, the helicopter tracks a group of men, some of whom the helicopter fliers say are armed. That understanding turned out to be not wholly true. A military spokesperson later told Reuters: "during the engagement, the helicopter mistook a camera for a rocket-propelled grenade launcher." The people were civilians, two of whom worked for Reuters news service. Two of the people wounded were children. "Well, it's their fault for bringing their kids into a battle," one of the American fliers is heard to say on the video.

After the video was released, *Wired* spoke with an ex-Army specialist who had been involved in a firefight on a neighboring street and arrived at the scene of the Apache helicopter soon after the civilians had been killed or wounded. He explained what he saw and heard from the video: some, though not all, of the people who were shot were carrying weapons, and the helicopter fliers' comments were "coping mechanisms," dark humor used to help them get through scary situations. He said a lot of soldiers are upset the video is public, because it shows some of them in one tense situation. It made them look callous, when in reality, most soldiers are not. Still, he didn't think WikiLeaks did a bad thing by

There's one, yeah.
Oh yeah.

Hotel Two-Six; Crazyhorse One-Eight.
Oh, yeah, look at those dead bastards.

Yeah, we won't shoot anymore.

Oh yeah, look at that. Right through the windshield!
Ha ha!

WikiLeaks has released videos of military actions.

posting the video. "I think it is good that they're putting this stuff out there." He said the video helps people ask questions about a "bigger picture:" "What are we doing there? We've been there for so long now and it seems like nothing is being accomplished whatsoever, except for we're making more people hate us."

The Manning Trial

During her trial, Manning told the court she leaked the information to spark public debate about the role of the military and about US foreign policy. As she later told the *New York Times Magazine*, "Let's protect sensitive sources. Let's protect troop movements. Let's protect nuclear information. Let's not hide missteps. Let's not hide misguided policies. Let's not hide history. Let's not hide who we are and what we are doing."

In March 2011, the US Army charged her with twenty-two counts relating to the unauthorized possession and distribution of more than 720,000 diplomatic and military documents. It was the largest leak in American history. She faced thirty-five years in prison. During his final days as president of the United States, Barack Obama commuted her sentence, meaning it ended then and there, only seven years in.

It wasn't an easy seven years Obama noted in his speech after freeing her. He said that if anyone thought she hadn't been punished, they were wrong. She lived in five different prisons. It was while inside that Manning announced she wanted to live as the female she knew she had been born as. This kicked off a long fight between her and the military for gender reassignment medical care. She went on a hunger strike and tried to kill herself twice. She faced strict punishments, like being forced to sleep naked, which a United Nations expert called "cruel" and "inhumane."

Obama also released Manning because Assange promised to turn in himself in to American authorities if her sentence was commuted. Assange has said he'll uphold his end of the bargain, but hasn't yet set a date to leave the Ecuadorian embassy in London.

The Aftermath

The Chelsea Manning example is powerful, showcasing a variety of reasons WikiLeaks could be loved or reviled. It changes everything, for the good and the bad. When once-secret information is published, the people involved are affected in all sorts of ways.

After her release from prison, Manning reentered the free world, changed in more ways than one. She behaves like many a whistle-blower: concerned, paranoid, and always on alert. When a *New York Times Magazine* reporter met her for an interview eight days after her release, she asked him to place his laptop inside a microwave, which would block radio waves and prevent spying.

The world was changed, too. According to many experts on both government as well as Manning's case, her actions represented a huge shift in the power of information and the perception of privacy—not to mention, the leak made Assange and WikiLeaks household names.

It also made Manning famous. She's now receiving notes from supporters in the most unlikely of places. One, from a fourteen-year-old boy who is transgender, said "You're an inspiration." Though Manning told the *New York Times Magazine* that she hadn't ever wanted to be a role model, she knew her life "would have been better," had she had an "inspiration" like that fourteen-year-old boy had.

In September 2017, Harvard's Institute of Politics invited Manning to be a visiting fellow. An uproar from the public about her being a traitor encouraged the university to rescind the invitation. Manning said on Twitter that she was "honored" to have been disinvited.

A Circle of Leaks and Responses

In 2007, WikiLeaks posted the US Army manual for soldiers working with prisoners at Camp Bucca, the largest United States detainee internment facility in Iraq. At the time of the leak, Camp Bucca imprisoned twenty thousand and was undergoing a $110 million expansion so that it could hold thirty thousand. Some of these prisoners were there because of yet another information leak: photos of abuse of prisoners at Abu Ghraib caused such a public response in 2004 that the United States military transferred all prisoners from Abu Ghraib to Camp Bucca. A few months later in 2007, WikiLeaks released information about Camp Delta, more commonly known as Guantanamo, in Cuba. Though the Camp Bucca operating procedures weren't great, they were better than Guantanamo's—so much so, that WikiLeaks said it hoped "detainees may be able to reveal the lack of military necessity in many Guantanamo procedures by comparing them to the Camp Bucca" procedures.

WikiLeaks and Scientology

In March 2008, only two years after Assange founded WikiLeaks, the organization released information on the Church of Scientology. Scientology is a body of religious beliefs developed by a writer in the 1950s. It is controversial, with lots of powerful followers, including many Hollywood celebrities. Critics consider it a brainwashing cult at worst, and at best, a clandestine organization based on falsehoods. To reveal its secrets would do considerable damage to a lot of people.

A former Church of Scientology employee gave WikiLeaks 208 pages of internal documents, dating from 1986 to 1992. They included instructions on ascending in rank in the church, evidence of church detectives tracking the travel plans of their critics, and evidence of how they gathered information on journalists to try to blackmail them into silence. Assange was attuned to this, in particular—according to *Complex*, he hated that the church had bullied hackers and publications in the name of secrecy for years.

These documents were meant for the eyes of only the highest-ranking Scientology officials, so the organization's response was swift. Within three days of the leak, they had requested the files be taken down; Assange responded by uploading even more documents.

Assange and Scientology

Interestingly, this was not the first time Assange and Scientology had gone head to head. In the late 1990s, he worked as a systems administrator for an Australian internet service provider (ISP). After a critic of Scientology anonymously leaked secretive internal documents on one of the chat forums the ISP hosted, Assange became involved. The church was furious—those documents were meant only for its highest-ranking members—and its lawyers asked Assange to supply them information about the ISP customer they suspected had leaked. Assange not only refused to do that, but he warned the person that the church was after him and published an anti-Scientology manifesto. In it, he said that Scientology's "worst critic at the moment is not a person, or an organization but a medium—the Internet. The Internet is, by its very nature, a censorship-free zone."

Sarah Palin's Emails

In September 2008, WikiLeaks posted emails from the personal email account of Republican vice-presidential candidate Sarah Palin. The justification for the leak was that Palin had used her Yahoo address to conduct professional business. While the leaked emails do show some correspondence between Palin and people at government email addresses, there wasn't much that made news. A lot of the leaked information was personal photos and friends' email addresses.

Even the alleged hacker—the person who came forward to claim responsibility for obtaining the emails that were then given to WikiLeaks to publish—was disappointed with the results. According to *Wired*, the hacker said that he found "nothing incriminating, nothing that would derail her campaign as I had hoped. All I saw was personal stuff, some clerical stuff from when she was governor … And pictures of her family."

The British National Party

Also in 2008, WikiLeaks posted a list of names, addresses, and occupations of people who belonged to the far-right British National Party (BNP). Police officers, senior members of the military, doctors, and professors were revealed to be a part of the racist political party. The BNP's politics have been called "fundamentally at odds" with the values of the British military, and it's illegal to be a member of the party and serve as a police officer. People were fired from their jobs after the list was published.

9/11

Government employees sent more than five hundred thousand text pager messages immediately before, during, and after the terrorist attacks of September 11, 2001. Anyone who used a text pager for their job—such as those working at the Pentagon, the New York Police Department, the Federal Bureau of Investigation (FBI), and the Federal Emergency Management Agency (FEMA)—might have sent a message to a colleague or loved one.

The following are two of these messages, unaltered—reproduced just as they looked when they were sent. The first appears to be someone (Chris) messaging a colleague about how phone signals were down or overloaded, and how another colleague (Jim at the FBI) didn't even know anything. Everyone was learning what was happening together, by watching the television news. The second message is full of heartfelt relief that a loved one was safe:

11:13:04 AM
Lines to Washington & Saudi are blocked or jammed. Couldn't get thru. Jim at the FBI had no info - he suggested we watch Fox or CNN. Chris.

5:20:30 PM
Honey wanted to tell you how much i love you. I was alittle worried.I Don't want to lose you now that I got you back. You mean everything to me. You have my whole heart and life. Ilove you so much,

From 3:00 a.m. on September 11, 2011 (the tenth anniversary of the attack) until 3:00 a.m. the following day, New York City time, WikiLeaks released the messages, each one synchronized to the time it was originally sent, ten years earlier. The organization wrote of its reason for releasing these messages: "The archive is a completely objective record of the defining moment of our time. We hope that its entrance into the historical record will lead to a nuanced understanding of how this event led to death, opportunism, and war."

Pieces of the Iraq War

American and British forces in Iraq were spotlighted when WikiLeaks published four hundred thousand classified military documents in October 2010. The *Guardian* called the revelations "a grim picture" of the two countries' involvement in torturing and killing, both by American and British hands, and by Iraqi military and police.

Some of the information detailed lying about reporting of data. For example, while officials from both the United States and Britain had said there was no official log of civilian deaths in the war, these leaked documents showed that there was a record kept. The death count was higher than expected. US authorities failed to investigate hundreds of reports of abuse, torture, rape, and murder by Iraqi police and soldiers.

One report documented an Apache helicopter shooting dead two Iraqi men who had been trying to surrender. The helicopter pilots were given the order to shoot because a lawyer back at their base, talking to them their headsets, told them "You cannot surrender to an aircraft," the *Guardian* reported. Chillingly, this helicopter was in the same military unit as the helicopter that killed civilians, including two Reuters employees later that year, and which was documented in a video given to WikiLeaks by Chelsea Manning.

DNC Email Leaks

In July 2016, WikiLeaks published almost twenty thousand emails from top officials in the US Democratic National Committee (DNC). Three months later, the organization followed up with two thousand emails hacked from DNC presidential candidate Hillary Clinton's campaign chairperson, John Podesta.

This tore the Democratic party apart at a key time: right in the middle of the presidential campaign season, mere weeks before the election.

In 2016, WikiLeaks released Democratic National Committee emails.

At the time of the first leak, Hillary Clinton and Bernie Sanders were in the running to be chosen as the Democratic nominee for president. The emails seemed to indicate the party was privately setting Clinton up to win. Because of the embarrassing content of the leaked emails, one day before the Democratic convention, the chair of the committee resigned. This added more stress to the situation.

Assange has stood by publishing the emails, even though they hurt only one party in the two-party election. The negative emails may have turned some voters toward the

Republican National Committee (RNC). Speaking to the *Intercepted* podcast, Assange said, "We specialize in really big scoops. You can't go, 'Oh, we have this massive scoop about corruption in the DNC. Now we need to balance this with a massive scoop about corruption in the RNC.'" He told the podcast he has nothing personal against Hillary Clinton and that he'd probably like her if they met in person.

In January 2017, the CIA concluded that Russian President Vladimir Putin had ordered the DNC emails to be hacked and then those emails given to WikiLeaks. The Russians didn't hand the emails directly to WikiLeaks but passed them through different channels until they reached the organization. This way, Assange could say he had not received political secrets from a foreign government. It was presumed that Russia did this because they wanted Republican candidate Donald Trump to win. Assange has always denied this.

The degree to which the leaked emails affected the election won't be known for a long time, if ever. A lot of variables were in play during the 2016 US presidential election. It's likely that a combination of them caused Trump to win the presidency and Clinton to lose. Many people think Assange shouldn't have released negative information about only one political party at such a crucial moment in the election. If he hadn't, he wouldn't have been staying true to WikiLeaks' mission: to shed light on what happens behind closed doors. What is more justifiably concerning is Assange's possible ties to Russia. If he knowingly accepted and published a leak from a foreign government, he could be charged with criminal activity.

After the second leak, the RNC's candidate for president, Donald Trump, tweeted: "I love WikiLeaks." Half a year later, Trump was the American president. His attorney general, Jeff Sessions, was calling for Assange to be extradited to the United States. Is Assange a hero or a villain? It really does depend on who you ask—and when.

Opposition

Assange's hero-or-villain status can be seen in the ways friends and foes try to support him or take him down. In some cases, they do both. Assange and WikiLeaks can inspire admiration, hate, and a mix of both emotions.

Anonymous

Anonymous is a hacker collective most publicly recognizable as people in Guy Fawkes masks. Fawkes was a Catholic dissident who plotted against the British government in the early 1600s. The mask, an artistic interpretation of his face, has come to stand for rebellion. With members of Anonymous hailing from all political parties, countries, and other demographics, it intends to be for anyone. They seek "anti-oppression," a former member told ABC News, by protecting free speech and fighting against government control. Members plan operations online and then crash Web servers, deface websites, and leak hacked information.

Since 2012, Anonymous has distanced itself from WikiLeaks, though the two groups have shared commonalities, including common enemies like the Church of Scientology, and have even respected one another. Anonymous members

People working as Anonymous often wear Guy Fawkes masks.

would often show up to public, in-person announcements by Assange and would attack WikiLeaks critics online.

However, as Assange sought political asylum for personal and professional reasons, Anonymous said WikiLeaks was "the one-man Julian Assange show." They felt the news that WikiLeaks was making pertained more to Assange having dinner with celebrities than to publishing information. When WikiLeaks started requiring donations in exchange for the viewing of information, Anonymous said it feared the freedom of information was taking a back burner for WikiLeaks.

Even still, according to the *Guardian*, Anonymous stands by its one-time friend when it comes to an even bigger force trying to take away its rights. "It goes without saying that we oppose any plans of extraditing Julian to the USA. He is a content provider and publisher, not a criminal," Anonymous said in a statement in 2012.

"Hactivist for Good"

In November 2010, a hacker calling himself "Jester" said he took down the WikiLeaks site and succeeded in keeping it dark for several hours. Just as WikiLeaks is perfectly timed in its release of information to have the most impact possible, this self-described "hactivist for good" took the website down right before it was to post hundreds of thousands of classified diplomatic cables sent between American officials. According to CNN, Jester said he took the controversial site down "for attempting to endanger the lives of our troops, 'other assets' & foreign relations." WikiLeaks' longtime connection with hackers doesn't mean all of them are on the organization's side.

Money, Money, Money

Even WikiLeaks uses credit cards. In 2011, Bank of America, VISA, MasterCard, PayPal, and Western Union all stopped doing business with the organization. WikiLeaks lost 95 percent of its revenue. Anyone who wanted to give the organization money, couldn't—not easily, at least, with all of those common forms of money transferring and payment gone. MasterCard was the first to end the blockade, in 2013.

The "Self-Aggrandizing FBI Executive"

Since he entered the public eye, Julian Assange has been considered both a hero and a villain. Which one he is depends on whom you ask—and maybe even what mood you catch that person in. People can sometimes see the positive in his actions and sometimes the negative.

When a man named Mark Felt entered the public eye, also for making government secrets public, he was instantly praised. He continues to be considered a hero today, though some are starting to wonder if he should be.

On Sunday, June 18, 1972, Bob Woodward was a twentysomething reporter at the *Washington Post*. He was only about three years into his career. With an early-morning phone call from his editor, he landed the biggest story of his life, what would become one of the biggest stories in America's modern history.

The night before, five well-dressed men carrying eavesdropping equipment were arrested inside the

Democrats' national headquarters at the Watergate office building. Together with colleague Carl Bernstein, Woodward started covering what seemed to be a plot to bug one of the country's two major political parties.

Woodward knew he needed an inside source who'd leak information. One of his first phone calls was to Mark Felt, a high-ranking official in the FBI. The two had met a couple of years before and kept in touch.

Woodward and Bernstein began investigating what would come to be known as Watergate. To write his articles, Woodward kept reaching out to his close source in the FBI. Felt kept answering, anxiously and, at times, reluctantly. In early August, he told the journalist it wasn't safe for them to talk in public or on the phone. They devised signals to send each other. When Felt had important information to share or Woodward had urgent questions to ask, one could signal the other, and they would meet at a predetermined private location away from both their homes and workplaces.

Because of these top-secret discussions, Felt became Woodward and Bernstein's Deep Throat. That was the nickname the journalists gave the whistle-blower within the government who helped them to crack the Watergate case. All three wanted Felt to remain anonymous in the newspaper articles. Decades later, in 2005, ninety-one-year-old Felt admitted he had been the informant.

In a 2005 *Washington Post* article on his relationship with Felt, Woodward wrote with nothing but fondness for the man. Among other positive attributes, Felt was always interested in helping Woodward, even at the tensest moments of the investigation. "Felt perhaps tolerated my aggressiveness and pushy approach because he had been the same way himself when he was younger," Woodward wrote. In addition to paying it forward by helping Woodward out as he had once been helped, or at least empathetic to Woodward's situation, Felt also talked to the reporter because of his love of country. "The threat to the integrity and independence of the bureau [the FBI] was real and seemed uppermost in his mind," Woodward wrote. He and Bernstein theorized that Felt leaked information to them because he "was trying to protect the office, to effect a change in its conduct before all was lost."

Unlike Assange, who's receiving the royal hero treatment and the lowly villain experience at the same time, Felt has been seen as nothing but a hero since Watergate. A 2017 *Politico* article suggests that all the documents that are now available clearly show a different side of the Watergate whistle-blower. Felt was a "duplicitous" man, "self-serving," whose FBI colleagues called him the White Rat. Whichever view of Felt is true, or even if they both are, the question remains: does it matter? Whistle-blowers can save the world, even if they can't save themselves.

As of 2017, Mike Pompeo is the Director of the Central Intelligence Agency.

Looking Ahead

I n many ways, Assange's and WikiLeaks's combined story is still unfolding. The legacy of the two is apparent, with new whistle-blowers stepping forward. New "-leaks" sites are serving niche markets and are becoming new attempts at pushing the boundaries of the law.

Edward Snowden

In 2013, Edward Snowden, who had worked for both the CIA and the federal government, copied and leaked National Security Agency (NSA) information. Almost immediately, he went on the move and received asylum from Russia. There are lots of connections between WikiLeaks and Snowden, including misperceptions—it's often assumed

Snowden leaked to WikiLeaks—and truths, such as that the website helped Snowden escape US authorities.

Snowden has said he was on his way to Ecuador when a freeze on his passport stuck him on his layover in Russia. Assange has told reporters that he had advised Snowden to go to Russia instead of Latin America, because he'd be safer there. Snowden met with Russian officials, and his WikiLeaks contact went with him.

Perhaps what's most interesting is how Assange has set the stage for Snowden just in his way of being in the world. Why not be a celebrity? This is how a whistle-blower could be. Assange has a larger-than-life personality that he continues to use to his advantage, even while living in tiny, residential quarters at an embassy. When *Wired* profiled Snowden, the online magazine found him to be "a uniquely postmodern breed of whistle-blower." Whereas Assange only seems like a magical man behind the curtain, Snowden kind of is: he regularly "appears" at conferences or awards events in video form. For a TED interview, his face was on a small screen, which was placed on two leg-like poles attached vertically to remote-controlled wheels. Snowden "walked" around the event, talking and posing for selfies.

No Longer the Only Kid on the Block

By 2011, not even five years since WikiLeaks launched its game-changing service, several copycat sites were trying to follow its lead. In April of that year, a *Forbes* reporter had counted all the sites that not only solicited leaked or stolen documents for publication, but also used the "leaks" suffix

Edward Snowden leaked government documents in 2013.

WikiLeaks has inspired many other "-Leaks" websites.

(that is, "SomethingLeaks"), just as WikiLeaks does. He counted twenty.

There were generic ones: CorporateLeaks. There were intriguing-sounding ones: PirateLeaks. There were region-specific, city-specific, and even university-specific ones, like BalkanLeaks, BrusselsLeaks, and JumboLeaks. (That last one is rather clever—it's for Tufts University, in Massachusetts, whose mascot is Jumbo the elephant. Education-centered leak sites are their own creature. UniLeaks has argued that since institutions of higher education receive public funding, their curtains, doors, and books should be open to the public to review.) ThaiLeaks and TuniLeaks mirror actual WikiLeaks documents in countries that block the original WikiLeaks.

Assange told *Forbes* he was fine with other sites starting up to do the same or similar work. "The supply of leaks is very large." But the reporter found that while the amount of information may be vast, the amount of leaked information actually isn't. He quoted the tweet of another writer, from the *Nation*: "the new era of leaks" is "missing just one thing: leaks."

The sites that seemed to do the best were focused niche markets. BalkanLeaks, for example, had shared "serious new material" for its region of the world. BrusselsLeaks is about more than just the Belgium city for which it's named: its focus is on the headquarters of the European Union.

Also of interest were the sites that were looking to reinvent the model WikiLeaks established. OpenLeaks is the brainchild of Daniel Domscheit-Berg, who used to work for WikiLeaks. He and a few others quit because they found Assange's leadership style "despotic," according to MemeBurn. Together, they started OpenLeaks, with Domscheit-Berg at the helm and a person known as "the architect" programming it. They do not present the documents raw and whole to the media, but rather curate them—verifying and sifting, picking and choosing what to share—and then hand them over.

AJTransparency is a secure platform on which whistle-blowers in the Arab world can submit information directly to the Middle East media giant, Al Jazeera. The organization receiving the information and perhaps posting it, is also the respected journalistic service that will fact-check before publishing. Its first big leak was the Palestine Papers, which comprised more than 1,600 documents about negotiations between the Israeli government and Palestinian Authority.

GlobalLeaks has made incredible use of the technology available. According to MemeBurn, the site allows information to pass anonymously, traveling in pieces. If one section, or node, gets shut down, that disruption doesn't affect the whole piece of information. Its open-source software, Tor Project, continues to make the process anonymous.

New Ways of Policing the News

Whatever the opinion of the role of WikiLeaks and its famous founder, Assange, it's certain they have impacted journalism. WikiLeaks works with more than one hundred major media outlets around the world to release its information to the public. Media policy and culture experts say WikiLeaks has affected how journalists work as well as philosophical issues related to journalism. There is also the matter of how the law may change its views of journalism, thanks to WikiLeaks.

The US Department of Justice has said it would like to press charges against Assange for some of WikiLeaks's publications, including the materials it got from Chelsea Manning, the two hundred fifty thousand State Department "Cablegate" documents, and even materials that detail how the CIA itself hacks computer systems.

If the US government does prosecute, it will be doing something never before done in the country: going after a news source simply for publishing truthful information. AlterNet, an online news magazine, said that the Espionage

Act is one law that is vague enough in its wording to be applied to Assange. However, using that would be an uphill battle for the government to win.

Unlike Chelsea Manning, who was a government employee and therefore required to keep documents secret and could be charged and tried accordingly, Assange is bound by no rules. A human rights lawyer helping Assange said the United States has "never really successfully prosecuted a nongovernment official for taking documents that were classified." The government certainly has never prosecuted a publisher, which Assange can be called, to this end.

Think back to the Pentagon Papers, the last time a similar case, in subject and size, was brought before the courts. The government lost; the newspapers fighting on the other side won their right to use their freedom of the press. Interestingly, a lawyer who worked on the Pentagon Papers case, First Amendment lawyer Floyd Abrams, didn't seem to know it would be an easy win for Assange either. An espionage charge would require proof that Assange had intended to harm the United States or help another country, which would be difficult for the government to prove beyond a reasonable doubt, experts have said. Abrams suggested that Assange has said things that make him sound like he has "a desire to undermine US foreign policy, comments that could backfire on him in court." Abrams said that as much as WikiLeaks' First Amendment argument is strong, so is the government's argument that WikiLeaks has caused "a genuine and serious national security argument."

anonymizing Making something anonymous, removing its connection from a known real person or thing.

cable A diplomatic or embassy cable is a confidential message between a country's consulate and its foreign ministry.

Cablegate The nickname for the 2010 release of 250,000 top-secret US documents by WikiLeaks. Since the Watergate scandal of the early 1970s, "-gate" has become a common suffix to describe an event as scandalous.

classified While there is flexibility in this term, it often means information whose release could seriously damage national security.

confidential While there is flexibility in this term, it generally means information whose release could damage national security.

extradition Handing someone who has been accused of a crime to the jurisdiction in which the crime took place.

False Claims Act (FCA) US federal legislation that says a private citizen may sue a person or business that is defrauding the government.

hacker An expert at computer programming and problem-solving. Sometimes the term is used negatively to mean a person who illegally accesses and sometimes tampers with a computer system.

handle A nickname.

infographic A visual image such as a chart or diagram used to represent information or data.

kickback A payment made to someone who has facilitated a transaction, usually an illegal or unethical one; often, a bribe.

leak The sharing of previously secret information.

political asylum Protection, often by a government other than the asylum seeker's home government, because the person is involved in political activities that may cause them harm.

qui tam A Latin term now used to mean "whistle-blower."

redact Remove or hide information, such as a name or home address, for legal or safety reasons before a document is published.

unclassified Documents not designated as secret.

whistle-blower A person who reveals a secret.

695 CE
The first law to protect whistle-blowers is issued.

1773
Benjamin Franklin becomes the first
well-known American whistle-blower.

1863
The False Claims Act, protecting and paying
whistle-blowers, passes in the United States.

1971
The first of the Pentagon Papers is published.

1971
Julian Assange is born in Australia.

1986
The False Claims Act is amended.

Chronology

2006

Julian Assange founds WikiLeaks.

2010

Thanks to whistle-blower Chelsea Manning, WikiLeaks releases tens of thousands of documents and other information relating to the Afghan war.

2010

Interpol puts Assange on its most-wanted list.

2012

Assange files for political asylum at the Ecuadorian embassy in London.

2017

Charges against Assange are dropped, but he remains in the embassy.

Books

Assange, Julian. *Julian Assange: The Unauthorised Autobiography*. Edinburgh, UK: Canongate Books, 2001.

———. *Cypherpunks: Freedom and the Future of the Internet*. New York: OR Books, 2016.

———. *When Google Met WikiLeaks*. New York: OR Books, 2016.

de Lagasnerie, Geoffroy. *The Art of Revolt: Snowden, Assange, Manning*. Stanford, CA: Stanford University Press, 2017.

Nance, Malcolm. *The Plot to Hack America: How Putin's Cyberspies and WikiLeaks Tried to Steal the 2016 Election*. New York: Skyhorse Publishing, 2016.

WikiLeaks. *The WikiLeaks Files: The World According to US Empire*. New York, Verso, 2016.

Videos

Trailer for *The Fifth Estate*

https://www.youtube.com/watch?v=ZT1wb8_tcYU

This summarizes the plot of a major motion picture about Assange and WikiLeaks. Assange did not approve of it.

Who is Julian Assange?

http://www.cnn.com/2017/01/05/politics/who-is-julian-assange-wikileaks/index.html

A brief CNN Politics video introducing Assange.

Websites

BBC News

http://www.bbc.com/news/world-11047811

A debate on whether or not Assange is a campaigner or attention-seeker.

The New Yorker

https://www.newyorker.com/magazine/2010/06/07/no-secrets

"Julian Assange's mission for total transparency."

WikiLeaks

https://wikileaks.org

This is the website for Assange's organization.

Agence France-Presse (AFP). "Does the US have a
    case against Julian Assange?" Alternet. Last accessed
    September 2017. http://www.alternet.org/rss/
    breaking_news/1003054/does_the_us_have_a_case_
    against_julian_assange.

———. "Mother of Julian Assange Fears for His Safety."
    The Swedish Wire, December 2, 2010. http://www.
    swedishwire.com/global-news/7458-mother-of-
    julian-assange-fears-for-his-safety.

Bamford, James. "The Most Wanted Man in the World:
    Behind the Scenes with Edward Snowden." *Wired*,
    August 2014. https://www.wired.com/2014/08/
    edward-snowden.

"A Brief History of Whistleblowers from Way Back."
    BuzzFeed, September 3, 2013. https://www.buzzfeed.
    com/fifthestate/a-brief-history-of-whistleblowers-
    from-way-back?utm_term=.ayPK2NWl9#.
    fk5E19e58.

"Chelsea Manning: Wikileaks Source and Her Turbulent
    Life." BBC, May 16, 2017. http://www.bbc.com/
    news/world-us-canada-11874276.

Davies, Nick, Jonathan Steele, and David Leigh. "Iraq War Logs: Secret Files Show How US Ignored Torture." *Guardian*, October 22, 2010. https://www.theguardian.com/world/2010/oct/22/iraq-war-logs-military-leaks.

Ellsberg, Daniel. "Why the Pentagon Papers Matter Now." *Guardian*, June 13, 2011. https://www.theguardian.com/commentisfree/cifamerica/2011/jun/13/pentagon-papers-daniel-ellsberg.

Erlanger, Steven, and Christina Anderson. "Julian Assange Rape Inquiry is Dropped but His Legal Problems Remain Daunting." *New York Times*, May 19, 2017. https://www.nytimes.com/2017/05/19/world/europe/julian-assange-sweden-rape.html?mcubz=3.

Green, Richard Allen, and Nicola Hughes. "'Hactivist for Good' Claims WikiLeaks Takedown." CNN, November 29, 2010. http://www.cnn.com/2010/US/11/29/wikileaks.hacker/index.html.

Greenberg, Andy. "TooManyLeaks: A List of Twenty WikiLeaks Copycats." *Forbes*, April 8, 2011. https://www.forbes.com/sites/ andygreenberg/2011/04/08/toomanyleaks-a-list-of- twenty-wikileaks-copycats/#56cc704547d9.

Hahn, Jason Duaine. "Before 'Going Clear,' WikiLeaks Was One of Scientology's First Major Threats." *Complex*, March 29, 2015. http://www.complex. com/pop-culture/2015/03/scientology-going-clear- wikileaks.

Halliday, Josh. "Anonymous distances itself from WikiLeaks." *Guardian*, October 12, 2012. https://www.theguardian.com/technology/2012/ oct/12/anonymous-distances-itself-wikileaks.

Holland, Max. "The Myth of Deep Throat." *Politico*, September 10, 2017. http://www.politico.com/ magazine/story/2017/09/10/watergate-deep-throat- myth-mark-felt-215591.

Holland, Patrick. "What Is WikiLeaks?" CNET, March 14, 2017. https://www.cnet.com/how-to/what-is- wikileaks.

Khatchadourian, Raffi. "No Secrets." *New Yorker*, June 7, 2010. https://www.newyorker.com/ magazine/2010/06/07/no-secrets.

———. "Julian Assange: A Man without a Country." *New Yorker*, August 21, 2017. https://www.newyorker. com/magazine/2017/08/21/julian-assange-a-man-without-a-country.

Kwek, Glenda. "Magnet for trouble: how Assange went from simple island life to high-tech public enemy number one." *The Sydney Morning Herald*, December 8, 2010. http://www.smh.com.au/technology/technology-news/ magnet-for-trouble-how-assange-went-from-simple-island-life-to-hightech-public-enemy-number-one-20101208-18pb3.html.

"911 tragedy pager intercepts." WikiLeaks. Last accessed September 2017. https://911.wikileaks.org.

Rauhala, Emily. "Sticks and Stones: The Top 5 Cablegate Insults." *Time*, November 29, 2010. http://newsfeed. time.com/2010/11/29/sticks-and-stones-the-top-5-cablegate-insults.

Reuters Staff. "Leaked U.S. video shows deaths of Reuters' Iraqi staffers." Reuters, April 5, 2010. http:// www.reuters.com/article/us-iraq-usa-journalists/ leaked-u-s-video-shows-deaths-of-reuters-iraqi-staffers-idUSTRE6344FW20100406.

Scahill, Jeremy. "Exclusive: Julian Assange Strikes Back at CIA Director and Talks Trump, Russia, and Hillary Clinton." The Intercept, April 19, 2017. https://

theintercept.com/2017/04/19/assange-strikes-back-at-cia-and-talks-trump-russia-and-hillary-clinton.

"A Selection from the Cache of Diplomatic Dispatches." *New York Times*. Last updated June 19, 2011. http://www.nytimes.com/interactive/2010/11/28/world/20101128-cables-viewer.html#report/cables-06MOSCOW9533.

Sevasti, Amanda. "The other WikiLeaks: 8 whistleblowing sites you probably don't know about." MemeBurn, June 14, 2011. https://memeburn.com/2011/06/8-whistle-blowing-sites-you-probably-didn%E2%80%99t-know-about.

Shaer, Matthew. "The Long, Lonely Road of Chelsea Manning." *New York Times Magazine*, June 12, 2017. https://www.nytimes.com/2017/06/12/magazine/the-long-lonely-road-of-chelsea-manning.html?mcubz=3.

Sontheimer, Michael. "'We Are Drowning in Material,'" *Spiegel Online*, July 20, 2015. http://www.spiegel.de/international/world/spiegel-interview-with-wikileaks-head-julian-assange-a-1044399.html.

Spiegel Staff. "The US Diplomatic Leaks: A Superpower's View of the World." *Spiegel Online*, November 28, 2010. http://www.spiegel.de/international/world/the-us-diplomatic-leaks-a-superpower-s-view-of-the-world-a-731580.html.

Week Staff. "WikiLeaks' 'Cablegate' Dump: 10 Biggest Revelations." *Week*, November 29, 2010. http://theweek.com/articles/488953/wikileaks-cablegate-dump-10-biggest-revelations.

"Whistleblowing History Overview." Whistleblowers International. Accessed September 2017. https://www.whistleblowersinternational.com/what-is-whistleblowing/history.

"WikiLeaks's Julian Assange suffered 'tragic' childhood." *Mail & Guardian*, January 15, 2011. https://mg.co.za/article/2011-01-15-wikileakss-julian-assange-suffered-tragic-childhood.

Woodward, Bob. "How Mark Felt Became 'Deep Throat.'" *Washington Post*, June 20, 2005. https://www.washingtonpost.com/politics/how-mark-felt-became-deep-throat/2012/06/04/gJQAlpARIV_story.html.

Zetter, Kim. "Palin E-Mail Hacker Says It Was Easy." *Wired*, September 18, 2008. https://www.wired.com/2008/09/palin-e-mail-ha.

———. "U.S. Soldier on 2007 Apache Attack: What I Saw." *Wired*, April 20, 2010. https://www.wired.com/2010/04/2007-iraq-apache-attack-as-seen-from-the-ground.

Page numbers in **boldface** are illustrations.

Index

Kristin Thiel lives in Portland, Oregon, where she is a writer and editor of books, articles, and documents for publishers, individuals, and businesses. She has worked on many of the books in the So, You Want to Be A… series, which offers career guidance for kids and is published by Beyond Words, an imprint of Simon & Schuster. She was the lead writer on a report for her city about funding for high school dropout prevention. Thiel has judged YA book contests and managed before-school and after-school literacy programs for AmeriCorps VISTA.